CRAZY-O-METER

TEN DANGEROUS SPORTS

by Noah Leatherland

BEARPORT PUBLISHING

Bearport Books, an imprint of Bearport Publishing by FlutterBee

Credits
All images are courtesy of Shutterstock.com, unless otherwise specified. With thanks to Getty Images, Thinkstock Photo, and iStockphoto.

Cover and title page,© Gregory Johnston, Master1305, SOMA surf-therapy, Khemmarach; Background pattern throughout, © topform; 2–3, © Ev. Safronov; 4–5, © Evgeniya Litovchenko, Valerii_M, Strahil Dimitrov, Dziewul; 6–7, © MarcelClemens, Sergei Bachlakov, Ihor Biliavskyi; 8–9, © Chinch, GlennV, MWiklik; 10–11, © Kirk Wester, AlexanderTrou, Magicleaf, EpicStockMedia, Chris Aschenbrener/Getty Images; 12–13, © marinat197, Jai Agnish, kevin brine, Zoran Milic, Panda Vector; 14–15, © Aleksei Lazukov, Mind Pixell, Jason S. Osborne, Gregory Johnston, Solomon Thompson; 16–17, © JoeSAPhotos, Khvost; 18–19, © Ev. Safronov, Aletkina Olga, Arden_Panikk, Calreyn88, CC0, via Wikimedia Commons; 20–21, © Sinesp, Hazan, Ihor Biliavskyi; 22–23, © TaviT, PradeepGaurs, IGORdeyka.

Bearport Publishing Company Product Development Team
Kayla Eggert, Theresa Emminizer, Kim Jones, Allison Juda, Cole Nelson, Naomi Reich, Steve Scheluchin, Tiana Tran

Library of Congress Cataloging-in-Publication Data is available at www.loc.gov or upon request from the publisher.

ISBN: 979-8-89577-605-6 (hardcover)
ISBN: 979-8-89577-693-3 (ebook)

For more information, write to Bearport Publishing, 3500 American Blvd W, Suite 150, Bloomington, MN 55431.
Printed in the United States of America.

CONTENTS

DANGEROUS SPORTS

Sports can be packed with fun and excitement. Sometimes, extreme sports can also quickly become unsafe. Let's take a look at some truly dangerous sports. How risky do they get?

WHITE WATER RAFTING

BEGAN: **1800s** SAFETY GEAR: **Life jacket and helmet**

Riding a raft doesn't seem that dangerous. But what if it involves paddling down rushing waterways? Between strong currents and jagged rocks, this is no calm afternoon sail. Riders could fall out and drift away!

Luckily, death is not common during white water rafting.

BMX

BEGAN: **1960s–1970s**
SAFETY GEAR: **Helmet, pads, braces**

What do you do when you fall off your bike? You get back up! But for BMX riders, the recovery might take a little longer.

BMX racing is the Olympic sport with the highest chance of injury.

BMX riders zoom around a track filled with **obstacles**. Going superfast makes it difficult to dodge things. Not to mention that many bikes don't have brakes. So, riders can't stop themselves from speeding headfirst into obstacles or other riders.

DOWNHILL SKIING

BEGAN: **8000–7000 BCE**

SAFETY GEAR: **Helmet, goggles, and waterproof jacket**

From loose rocks to other snow-lovers, skiers have so many things to watch out for while racing down the slopes. Sometimes, there are even **avalanches**!

Some skiers wear avalanche airbag backpacks that inflate in case of a disaster.

One of the greatest risks of skiing is losing control and hitting trees at fast speeds. Skiers might get broken bones or worse. Hitting trees is the most common cause of death in skiing!

SURFING

BEGAN: **Around 3000 BCE**
SAFETY GEAR: **Surfboard leash and wetsuit**

Some of the most common **injuries** surfers get come from their own surfboards. After nasty **wipeouts**, the edges of boards can bang surfers up with cuts and bruises.

But that doesn't mean the waters aren't also dangerous. Strong ocean currents can pull surfers away from shore. Huge waves may hold riders underwater and drown them.

Surfers must also look out for sea life. Jellyfish, seals, and sharks can all be a threat.

ICE HOCKEY

BEGAN: **1600s**
SAFETY GEAR: **Helmet and padding**

Ice hockey players are sometimes too focused on the puck to pay attention to what's around them. They may crash into goal posts or the boards. *Ouch!*

However, the biggest dangers on the ice are the players themselves. The sharp blades on their skates can cause horrible cuts. Some people have died from getting sliced in the neck by the metal blades!

Ice hockey players can also get whacked by other players' sticks.

CHEERLEADING

BEGAN: **1860s** SAFETY GEAR: **Rubber-soled shoes**

Do you like to fly? Cheerleaders do all kinds of extreme tricks in the air. But the real challenge is the landing . . . and making sure your teammates catch you in time.

Not landing these stunts safely can lead to broken bones and **concussions**. The worst falls can even **paralyze** cheerleaders. The athletes who are doing the throwing and catching are also at risk of being hit by flying limbs.

Around 30,000 cheerleaders are sent to the hospital with sports-related injuries every year.

FOOTBALL

BEGAN: **1800s**
SAFETY GEAR: **Helmet and padding**

Hut, hut, hike! Football is an extreme full-contact sport where players plow down opponents to score points. Often, this involves **tackling** and colliding with others on the field.

Players can twist their legs or sprain their arms when being tackled. The biggest danger of all is concussions. Serious injuries can have long-term effects that can not only cost the game but also risk players' careers.

Concussions can cause headaches, dizziness, and trouble speaking.

MOTORSPORTS

BEGAN: **Around 1880s** SAFETY GEAR: **Helmet and fire suit**

With so many cars zooming around the track, accidents are bound to happen in motorsports. Crashes are the most obvious cause of injuries and deaths.

Fast cars need a lot of fuel. So, when vehicles crash into one another, the gas can start a fire. The blast from the fire may harm anybody nearby. Even those watching from the sidelines are at risk of getting burned!

When cars crash into one another, it can cause a pileup.

BASE JUMPING

BEGAN: **1978** SAFETY GEAR: **Helmet, parachute, and wingsuit**

3 . . . 2 . . . 1 . . . Go! BASE jumpers take thrills to the extreme by leaping off the tallest things possible. Yet, faulty parachutes can make the sport go downhill very fast.

The world's highest BASE jump was done off the side of Mount Everest.

Bad weather is also dangerous. Strong winds or heavy rain can push jumpers off course, knocking them into cliffs or other objects on their way down.

FREE SOLOING

BEGAN: **1970s** SAFETY GEAR: **None**

Most rock climbers use safety **equipment** to help them along the way. But not free solo climbers. Free soloing is a sport that doesn't use any gear at all!

There is no room for mistakes when it comes to free soloing. One slip may mean instant death. Hot **temperatures** can make climbers feel tired—and they have no rope to help them rest!

One solo climber took 3 hours and 56 minutes to go up a tall rock formation in California.

GLOSSARY

avalanches large amounts of snow, ice, earth, or rock that slide down a mountainside

concussions brain injuries caused by heavy blows to the head

equipment helpful things that are used for certain activities or jobs

injuries harm done to people's bodies

obstacles things that block paths

paralyze to make a body or body system unable to move or work

tackling stopping someone by knocking them to the ground

temperatures how hot or cold things are

wipeouts when surfers fall off surfboards and into the water

INDEX